She Speaks in Verse

Whispers of Strength, Woven in Poetry

Sanaa Mehrotra

BlueRose ONE.com
Stories Matter
NewDelhi • London

BLUEROSE PUBLISHERS
India | U.K.

BlueRose ONE
Stories Matter
NewDelhi • London

For permissions requests or inquiries regarding this publication,
please contact:

BLUEROSE PUBLISHERS
www.BlueRoseONE.com
info@bluerosepublishers.com
+91 8882 898 898
+4407342408967

ISBN: 978-93-7018-181-6

Cover design: Shubham Verma
Typesetting: Sagar

First Edition: May 2025

Dedication

To those who feel deeply through words,
and to the emotions that flow from the soul to the page.

Contents

Author's Note

While some of these poems draw upon my personal emotions and experiences, many are inspired by the lives and stories of others, as well as the rich narratives found in various books and series. This collection is a tapestry woven from a multitude of perspectives and imaginative sources, capturing the essence of diverse inspirations.

From the Author
Dedication

To everyone who has wandered with me through the maze of my thoughts and feelings.

To my parents, for the endless love and the life lessons that stuck. For always being by my side however far down I spiral. This one's for all those times when dad's advice and mom's hugs worked wonders.

To my relatives, both far and close, this is for always taking care of me, spoiling me and loving me for the girl I am.

To my friends, a thank you for putting up with my random poetic ramblings. This one's for all the times I made you read a poem of mine mid-school.

To my heart, which insists on feeling everything way too deeply.

And to life's roller coaster — thanks for the material.

Chapter One

Legends of The Starry Enclave

from natural affinity, or fro
sympathy and manifesting i

Dreams **/dri:m/**

Events and feelings happ
while asleep. Aspirations
and goals for the future.

Dreamscapes

As your eyes flutter gently falling asleep,
You'll lose parts of you solemnly deep.
As slumber cages every part of your being,
Your dreams awake, far distant from the living.

Every thought and feeling put in a delicate dream,
From faded fantasies to nightmares that scream,
Will exist unbound by limits and thriving in creativity,
In this universe far away from the shackles of reality.

As your eyes flutter gently falling asleep,
Into another land you'll quietly seep.
As slumber cages every part of your being,
You'll exist in the world between the dead and living.

The Fallen Angel's Descent

The Frost has unfrozen over the gateways of hell,
But whom shall the innocent angel tell?
For there was nobody who would listen to her plight.
Thus, in silence, she faded from sight.

There's a gaping hole to hell itself she sees,
Avoiding sin, she thought, was ought to be an ease.
But there was nobody who would listen in heaven.
Thus, her wings were forever tragically broken.

The Enchanted Prison

You're stuck inside the pages of a book's fairy tale,
And here, the world seems so unfamiliar.
There's no escape, how much ever you shout or wail,
And until it engulfs you, you can't grasp it evermore.

Each step you take into the unknown will feel new,
From witches' curses to angels' unreal beauty,
You must forget everything that you once knew,
For the script unraveling here, is both raw and unruly.

The looming peril will drown your every sense,
And the dangers won't relent, not for a single defense.
Slowly, your left and right will steadily blur into the night,
And the threats won't wane, no matter how you fight.

Pearl Gates

Eyes, those which flood emotions engulfed by our soul,
Those which let out every feeling not crafted into speech.
The sight to the beautiful world keeping us whole,
The art of mastering the impossible, they teach.

The pupil, a realm of wonders seen so briefly,
Containing the rage of the harshest sea's cry,
Or the gentleness of the sky with clouds draped lovingly,
Or even the despondence of a dull night sky.

Eyes, those which we fall for, oh so ever easily,
Eyes, the core of hate and love, all alike,
Eyes, those we look into, with synchronized heartbeat adoringly,
Eyes, the pearl gates, to our heart's each and every strike.

angels

and

Death is not a lover

Oh yes he is.

death

Angels and Death

When the angels descend to save and bless,
I'd plead with them, I must confess.
And should death shred his wings in discontent,
I'd tell him, his time's awfully spent.

No, I wouldn't inflict such agony,
But if it were to happen, why halt the treachery?
No, I don't believe I'm too important,
For causing a war not so expectant.

When the angels descend to save and bless,
I'd beg them to leave and ignore my mess.
And should death shred his wings in discontent,
I'd tell him, I'm not useful enough for his resent.

The Anatomy of Unfairness

Flower petals wither away too,
When they're done all the way through,
Fragile wings of a butterfly will break one day,
When they let go and fly above, far, far away,

The heart craves some rest too,
From wounds that never healed all the way through.
The lungs grow weary of breathing away,
From the battle scars of air storms each day.

Even strength one day turns to fear,
Even hope one day will shed a tear.
Sometimes, the heart longs to feel fresh air,
Sometimes, the lungs wish to pump blood, all too unfair.

Chapter Two

Nature's Whispers

celestial shorelines

Celestial Shorelines

Like stardust adrift in the Milky Way,
A beach is shaped by sand of a golden shine.
The waves roar with a dance and sway,
And sandcastles destroyed leave a child to whine.

The feel of water all across your skin,
The feel of sand beneath your feet,
It loses you in the easiness to breathe in,
Where the soul and the heart effortlessly meet.

winter wonderland

Winter Wonderland

The winds bid farewell to warmth and grow colder,
As people huddle closer to sustain the frost.
Icicles shriek as everything grows harsher,
While grudges and anger from hearts are lost.

For it's the most wonderful time of the year,
As snowflakes fall and symbolize a new chance.
The power and beauty of the white landscape's sphere,
Is so that one can't look away from its luminous trance.

Winter, the bitter and best season of all, truly,
Always finds space in our hearts to spare.
To enlighten our spirits from all that's dreary,
So, Come on, it's time to put on layers and layers.

Ephemeral Wings

Ephemeral Wings

With wings beautiful as fairies aside,
Fluttering in the breezy wind's trance, they fly,
Carried away by the earth's own tide,
They often disappear, leaving us to wonder why.

From baby showers to funerals, you'd witness them alive,
From caterpillar to butterfly, they strive,
Captivated by each flutter as they thrive,
Linking the garden to the graveyard's life and death drive.

Beauty in Ruins

Why must the calm of nature always be seen,
When destruction and chaos exist just the same?
Why must waves and trees be described as serene,
When their rage and terror are far from tame?

There's beauty in the life-taking lava from a volcano,
And innocence in a surging, raging tsunami,
There's something pretty in poisonous ivy,
And something about a storm that's wildly lovely.

Hidden intimacy in all that's deemed terrible,
Concealed truths in every secret of the world,
A vibrance in each sound, distinctly verbal,
An elegance in each leaf and tendril tightly curled.

Meadows

Sunlight from the orb delves through the trees,
A stream morphed from the tears of the pain a goddess sees.
High and low, like the churning waves of the ocean,
The sunflower's tendrils through the meadows are woven.

Winds calmly breeze as if angels sigh in relief,
Like a picture framed, everything stagnant, even the frailest leaf.
Cotton candy clouds waver over the forlorn fields,
In the same second, a bee from petals' pixie dust yields,

When you need a place to hide within empty thoughts,
Everything in these mellow meadows provide comfort lots.
When you need time to be lost in imaginary worlds,
Nothing in these mesmerizing meadows denies the absurd.

how it weathers away

How it Weathers Away

When the first snowflake falls at dawn,
Will it all truly be gone?
When the last butterfly will fly,
Will it all truly die?

Slowly-slowly its fading away,
Slowly- slowly its dying everyday,
It weathers away like lily petals,
They fall, like autumn leaves settle,
And before it turns into something,
It will all turn into nothing.

The flowers are withering away,
It's gladdening that it ended this way,
Because if the flower bloomed,
Then truly would all be doomed.

When the first snowflake will fall,
Finished stands the built-up wall,
With the whole world in between
One day nothing it'll mean.

Because you can witness it weathering away,
Drowning a little more everyday,
One day it'll die,
It'll be too late by then,
goodbye.

Chapter Three

The Symphony of Existence

each passerby

Each Passerby

Can't help but smile at each passerby,

Can't help but strengthen every bonded tie,

For it's the beauty in the colours of black and white,

For it's the beauty of each soul hidden in plain sight.

Beauty

A vast subject it is, beauty,
Can never exist just finitely,
As the vision of the eyes,
Has different ways to tell lies.

A vast subject it is, beauty,
The ugly could be lovely,
Yet the lovely could be fake,
So, tear your heart off this stake.

Belief

What a person thinks from their heart,
Is what they'd like to believe,
What they felt at the very start,
Shapes what they'll later perceive.

First instincts branch through every nerve,
As blood from the heart fuels unnecessary emotions.
In the end, all abandon, but the brain will always serve,
So, why to the heart, all this prolonged devotion?

Truth and Dare

The world slowly fades away,
Into withering fragments once believed to stay.
Breaking into shards a little more every day,
And to delay the inevitable, there's nothing to say.

Letting go with hope there's more to come,
Tearing away from expectations of some,
Locked in a cage people call insane,
Keys to them morphed from dread and pain.

Lost in a world of lies breeding fake,
Need to pull the heart off a stake,
Lost in a world of truth far from real,
Need to stop having emotions to feel.

People say it's a life far from fair,
I say it's more like truth or dare,
People say it's a life far from true,
I say it's a game till it defeats you.

Little Lies

Her pupils dilate as she lets out a smile,
With evil thoughts lurking beneath her sweet words,
She lets out a perfect laugh once in a while,
Disguising the lies she confines on her tongue.

For after all, why should her wicked lies matter,
When there are always things people don't know?
For after all, who cares if all would shatter,
When there are always things never shown?

Miracles

When the hardest times of our lives are here,
All we can do is struggle and silently bear,
Pray and hope that somehow all will be alright,
And to the impossible, put on a good fight.

Sometimes, a presence can be sensed all around,
Yet in every corner you search, nothing to be found.
The feeling is soothing, like a whisper so tender,
Like a gentle assurance that brings sweet surrender.

Thrill's Edge

Red lights laugh at the thought of a rager,
Stop signs threaten the yearns for danger,
How it flows like venom through the veins,
How it keeps you bound by its reigns.

The feel of wind on your skin,
The feel of fear to let in,
Knowledge that one foreign move or action,
Might as well be your last decision.

Chapter Four

The Echoes of Emotions

whispers of loneliness

Whispers of Loneliness

Loneliness, a piercing sword into the heart,
Creeping through the corners of the veins,
Spreads in the soul slowly tearing it apart,
Caging all of you in invisible chains.

Every part of existence feels like a burden,
As if to living there's no continued purpose.
The rush of everything around feels forced and sudden,
As if life replicates the despair of missing your bus.

It slowly leaves you behind from the rest,
Mocking your inability to make it through.
Replicating the agitation on failing a test,
Feeling like the whole world is against you.

Echoes of Solitude

Why would one need other people to sustain?
Lose yourself to interlink with another,
In the long run, arises only dread and pain.
For a ruler rules solitary, like no other.

The blade of knife edges in singular motions,
Swords cut deeper with lonely jabs swiftly,
A gun thrives with just one bullet's devotion,
A lone shuriken pierces and shreds, harsh but deftly.

Because why would you need other people to live?
When you know you can be content anyway,
So why in the long run is there any other motive?
Beyond surviving another solitude day.

Perpetual Outcast

From the very beginning, it felt different,
Not in a way praised as unique,
But in the way misery bore the heart with a dent,
Turning life into a constant struggle.

Thoughts were not as simple as they seemed to appear,
The tongue held words too different and perhaps unjust.
The feeling, The fear of losing people and being lonely,
Will always gradually tear you apart from the rest.

Exclusion, a feeling not explained in mere phrases,
A cage with a key lost, forever not found,
A fragment of your soul behind sharp fences,
Makes you constantly question the thoughts of those around.

salty sorrows

Salty Sorrows

Like raindrops let go by forlorn clouds,
They stream down your face with emotions to bear,
Stinging as the pain vents from hidden wounds,
Piercing through each soul full of fear.

Oh, but aren't they like a beam of sunlight through the canopy,
The harbinger of ecstasy, too hard to contain,
Tears of happiness they're called, found quite rarely,
Showing that joy, too, can replace the pain.

Curved Bliss

A feeling hard to cage inside you,
Only conceived by a chosen few.
The joyous feel overwhelms your expression,
Your smile shines like a gold medal that you've won.

Happiness is in the little things all around,
Conquers you whole till no despair is found,
Happiness is in memories and people all around,
It's in the silent noise ringing loud in a smile's sound.

It helps you with each small step along the way,
Expresses warmth in every word you say,
A smile, a secret entrusted to people near,
Stitches wounds until they slowly disappear.

Alone Amidst All

When you're surrounded by people in every corner,
When friends and strangers all seem to gather,
Is it normal to feel so alone?
Is it normal for no one to earn your trust?

When you can make everyone laugh and smile,
When you have friends who supposedly make life worthwhile,
Is it normal to feel so empty inside?
Is it normal to have everybody but nobody by your side?

euphoria in verse

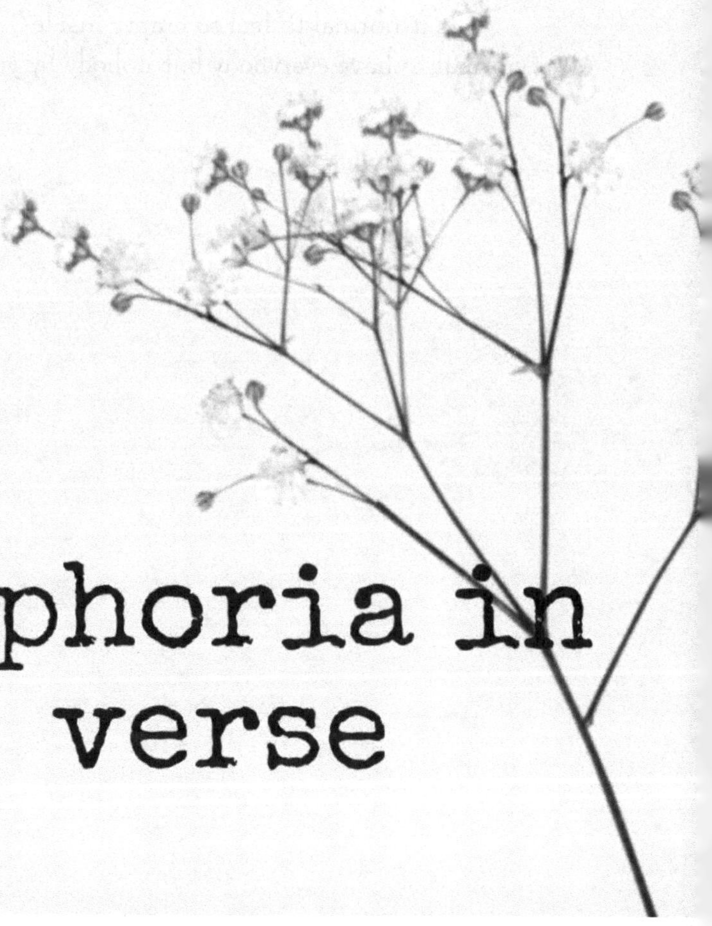

Euphoria in Verse

There's a glimmer in the meadows of despair,
Arising from the depths within,
A sprinkle of hope with love to spare,
With enough laughter to breathe in.

The feeling of ecstasy engulfs your soul,
Even as the thorns of a rose shred your back,
The rhythm of a beating heart captures you whole,
Until the knives of reality change your track.

addictive whispers

Addictive Whispers

The taste engraved on the soul of the tongue,
As numbness from obsession has start to sung,
Goes from just once more to every single day,
lingers and haunts till the day you lay.

For it's an evil entity, obsession that is,
A few seconds forth, it's the scent you'll miss.
For it traps every part of your entire being,
Leaves you in between the dead and the living.

Chapter Five

Struggles and Shadows

Easy

Is it supposed to be easy to let out a smile?
Because I haven't felt one for a while.
Is it supposed to be easy to let out laughter?
Because now, the throat just feels denser.

Another night, another day, not knowing,
Another fight, another way to end up crying,
Losing things that once brought joy,
Embracing failure, as if it's the only choice.

Only Me

Envy stridden glance at everyone all around,

No imperfection or struggle can be found,

So is it only me running to cope with time's agony?

So is it only me falling apart at life's misery?

Wander

Sometimes the eyes wander off to a distance,
And the brain is overtaken by a foreign entity,
As pain floods in every pleading glance,
The ache bleeds tears for mercy.

To be expelled to a place for from here,
Where there's only the choice to be alone.
A forced smile no longer needed to wear,
For there's nothing left to be shown.

Take the Gift

Oh lord of death and mercy, take them away,

Take the gift of life and it's beauty,

For their heart pains to stay,

At a place already killing them slowly.

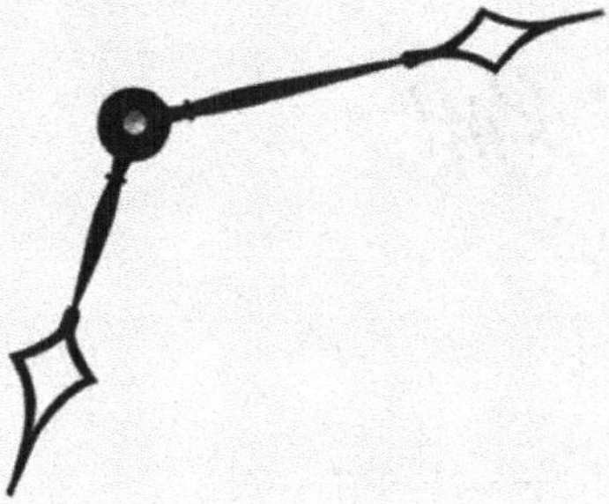

pressure

Pressure

Down, down, pressure throbs downward,
Pressure to be perfect therefore onward,
Hidden meanings behind words and disappointed frowns,
How can one go anywhere but down?

Down, down, pressure on its path to destroy people,
Pressure to be great, to be the best, beyond normal,
Your struggle unseen until you're lost out at sea.
It's the pressure to be how everyone wants you to be

Chapter Six

Their Forbidden Journey

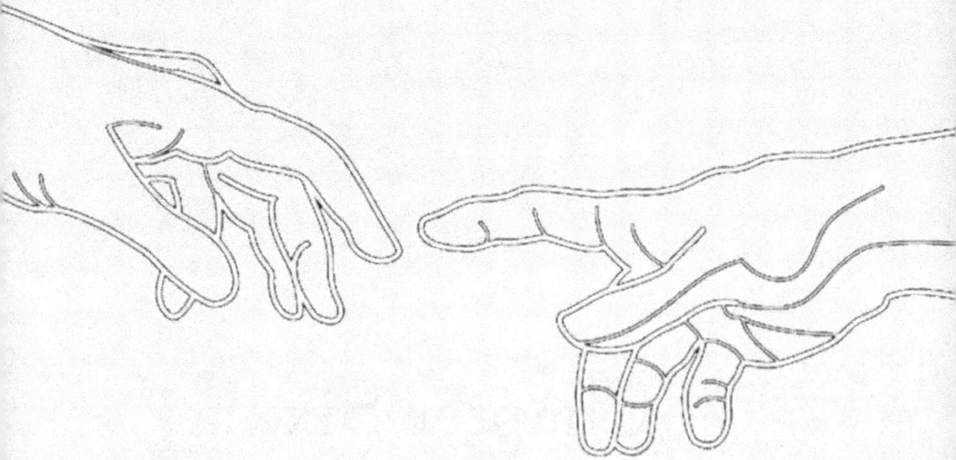

new love

New Love

if Romeo hadn't poison his vial when Juliet died,
Would he have found someone new to enlighten his life?
Could he have engraved a new smile into his soul?
Walk an aisle with vows crafted for his wife?

It's hard to say new love exists beyond fairy tales,
Because why would you leave your heart so frail?
When love already tore it apart the first time around,
Why would that miseric pain ever again want to be found?

Forbidden

She glances across the ballroom, her large blue eyes wide,
Her arms wrapped around her betrothed responsibility,
Yet her heartbeat for him she can't subside,
A cruel play of the universe tearing apart her symphony.

She can't disappoint the kingdom, she can't run away,
And he cannot lose his work for a forbidden girl.
The whispers and glances, what would people say?
For it's far from possible for them to understand she's his world.

Confessions to arisen anger and the slam of a door,
A princess abdicated from her palace forever.
The realisation hits, there's was nothing more
They wanted than to never let go of each other.

Run Away

They agreed to run away,
Forever with each other they'd be hidden,
Far from where their love couldn't stay,
Far away from the place boundation stridden.

But it was hard for her to run from responsibility,
To never see her blood and friends,
Yet for him, she was his heart and family
And he was prepared to stay with her till the very end.

Yet her heart yearned back home, she knew,
And slowly he could see the bitter truth,
Letting her go, he whispered "I'll always love you"
And tearfully, she went back along her route.

glances

Glances

Sneaking glances across the room,
It feels a bit too good to be true.
Loving her is a synonym to doom,
Because, well, he's not allowed to.

The way it feels to be in love again,
Is a mere distraction to how it'll feel later,
When all that will be left is pain,
Because he knows she deserves better.

One could say it's sweet, a mended heart,
Yet, it teeters on the brink of a breaking chance,
One could say it's cute, until it breaks them apart,
And so, for now, he sneaks another glance.

Hushed Voices

She wasn't welcomed back, at least not instantly,

In hushed disappointed tones they spoke of her betrayal,

Her return back home felt lonely,

Being glared at, slowly turned into the new normal.

Vows

They stand in the aisle, their eyes bonded,
As they take their vows for the rest of eternity,
The intensity of their words leaves the crowd astounded,
For not everyday such phrases are said so lovingly.

"I do." the groom softly said,
And she wrapped her arms around him swiftly,
As they embraced as if all but them were dead
And this was the start of their forever love story.

Chapter Seven

Seasons of Change

The Days That Didn't Last

The dainty days of the bittersweet past,
Threaten to spill from the overflowed memories,
Heart beating, holding on to what couldn't last,
Nostalgia, a cruel symphony reckons to tease.

The days when worries sounded a problem of the future,
When smiles and happiness were built into our nature,
And sleeping was the furthest things from our mind,
If only back to that time, we could rewind.

Now all we do is live in fragmented worry,
And frowns and disheartment tread killing the merry,
Sleeping now sounds like the best part of the day,
If only it could go back to when it wasn't this way.

Woven Farewells

Just two souls lost on their way,
Interconnected with more than the words they say.
Just the people who might never meet again,
Will forget they kept each other sane.

Just two people lost in the memories of the past,
Just another friendship destiny didn't let last,
Yes, bonds break and scatter away,
But still, hope enlightens for some to stay.

Their laughs connected, pretty smiles they wear,
Moments turn to memories as time sheds a tear,
All that can be done is watch the time fly,
Untill once again the time comes to say goodbye.

they
go
as
soon
as
they
come

They Go as Soon as They Come

People, so different from each other, yet so similar,
They enter your life with a beaming smile,
Sharing words, feelings & even laughter,
Yet uncertainty lurks, will they stay a while?

Looking in their eyes, feeling a sense of belonging & comfort,
You'd share a quick knowing glance across the room,
Not knowing the threads of time would shed to dirt,
Not knowing the warmth, ahead awaits doom.

One would ask, what is the point of such bonds then?
If they were just meant to be torn & pierced apart?
It's the memories meant to be cherished & deepened,
It's the memories to engrave in a reminiscing heart.

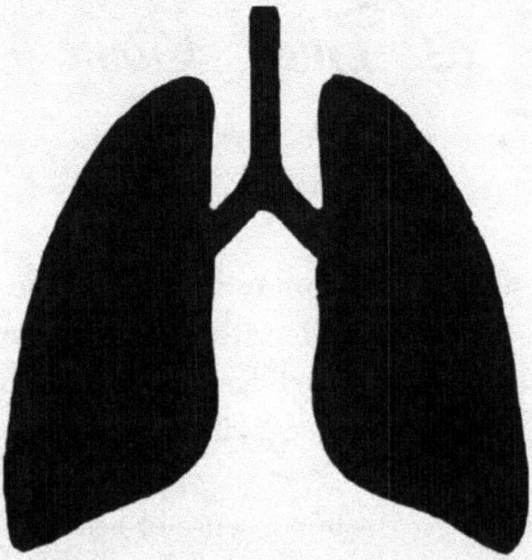

last breath

Last Breath

Like an old turtle on its last breath,
Has seen enough of life to not care about death.
Like a young bird born moments ago,
Can't wait to see what's next in life's flow.

Pleading to let the death of this come close,
Pleading for the farewell of these woes.
Begging to move on to a new chapter,
Begging to see what else life has to offer.

closing a chapter

Closing A Chapter

Once upon a time, in life's library, opened a book,
Very little space between thousands it took.
Yet it was literally the world for one,
Who's every chapter was engraved once done.

There was a chapter closer to the heart than the rest,
Letting go and closing it was the ultimate test.
But when the signs and time had come,
It shred and tore, giving pain impossible to numb.

Ultimately awoken was the toughest time of all,
To postpone the farewell, you could only stall.
Goodbyes therefore were bid, quite painfully,
Here's to hoping the new chapter will be just as lovely.

Chapter Eight

The End

me

Me

Just a girl with dreams,
Too big to contain.
Just a girl with a heart,
Too big to keep sane.

Hiding me away,
Till the storm subsides.
Calming the seas,
Ruled by my harsh tides.

Just a girl with the notion,
To conquer the big world.
Just a girl with undivided devotion,
Towards her own worth.

Hiding me away,
Until the flowers resurface.
Watering and nurturing growth,
While catching up to life's pace.

Final Thoughts:

As the final ink dries and the last page turns,
I leave you, with a piece of my soul.

These poems are not mere words, but breaths of my being and moments of my existence captured in time.

I have poured my joys, sorrows, dreams, and fears onto these pages, hoping they find a home within you.

May they resonate with your heart, stir your spirit, and accompany you in the quiet corners of your own life.
Thank you for allowing my thoughts to intertwine with yours.

As you close this book, carry a piece of it with you, and remember that in the vast complex way of life, our hearts will always have time for appreciating the small thoughts and feelings.

With heartfelt gratitude and a touch of bittersweet
Sadness,

Sanaa Mehrotra

Contact Information:

In this age of the digital sphere, I welcome your thoughts, reflections, and feelings from afar.
Connect with me and share your journey.
You can find me through the digital realms at sanaamehrotra4@gmail.com where you can tell me what your favourite poem was, what other kind of poems you'd like to read.

I wish a good day to every one of my readers.

✧･ﾟ: *✧･ﾟ:*THE END*:･ﾟ✧*:･ﾟ✧